My Most Beautiful Dream

Min allra vackraste dröm

A picture book in two languages

C000131896

Download audiobook at:

www.sefa-bilingual.com/mp3

Password for free access:

English: **BDEN1423**

Swedish: **BDSV2831**

Cornelia Haas · Ulrich Renz

My Most Beautiful Dream

Min allra vackraste dröm

Bilingual children's picture book,

with audiobook for download

Translation:

Sefâ Jesse Konuk Agnew (English)

Narona Thordsen (Swedish)

Lulu can't fall asleep. Everyone else is dreaming already – the shark, the elephant, the little mouse, the dragon, the kangaroo, the knight, the monkey, the pilot. And the lion cub. Even the bear has trouble keeping his eyes open ...

Hey bear, will you take me along into your dream?

Lulu kan inte somna. Alla andra drömmer redan – hajen, elefanten, den lilla musen, draken, kängurun, riddaren, apan, piloten. Och lejonungen. Även björnen kan nästan inte hålla ögonen öppna ...

Du björn, kan du ta med mig in i din dröm?

And with that, Lulu finds herself in bear dreamland. The bear catches fish in Lake Tagayumi. And Lulu wonders, who could be living up there in the trees?

When the dream is over, Lulu wants to go on another adventure. Come along, let's visit the shark! What could he be dreaming?

Och med det så finner sig Lulu i björnarnas drömland. Björnen fångar fisk i
Tagayumisjön. Och Lulu undrar, vem skulle kunna bo där uppe i träden?
När drömmen är slut vill Lulu uppleva ännu mer. Följ med, vi hälsar på
hajen! Vad kan han drömma om?

The shark plays tag with the fish. Finally he's got some friends! Nobody's afraid of his sharp teeth.

When the dream is over, Lulu wants to go on another adventure. Come along, let's visit the elephant! What could he be dreaming?

Hajen leker tafatt med fiskarna. Äntligen har han vänner! Ingen är rädd för hans spetsiga tänder.

När drömmen är slut vill Lulu uppleva ännu mer. Följ med, vi hälsar på elefanten! Vad kan han drömma om?

The elephant is as light as a feather and can fly! He's about to land on the celestial meadow.

When the dream is over, Lulu wants to go on another adventure. Come along, let's visit the little mouse! What could she be dreaming?

Elefanten är lika lätt som en fjäder och kan flyga! Snart landar han på den himmelska ängen.

När drömmen är slut vill Lulu uppleva ännu mer. Följ med, vi hälsar på den lilla musen! Vad kan hon drömma om?

The little mouse watches the fair. She likes the roller coaster best.
When the dream is over, Lulu wants to go on another adventure. Come
along, let's visit the dragon! What could she be dreaming?

Den lilla musen är på ett tivoli. Mest gillar hon berg- och dalbanan.

När drömmen är slut vill Lulu uppleva ännu mer. Följ med, vi hälsar på

draken. Vad kan hon drömma om?

The dragon is thirsty from spitting fire. She'd like to drink up the whole lemonade lake.

When the dream is over, Lulu wants to go on another adventure. Come along, let's visit the kangaroo! What could she be dreaming?

Draken är törstig av att ha sprutat eld. Hon skulle vilja dricka upp hela sockerdrickasjön.

När drömmen är slut vill Lulu uppleva ännu mer. Följ med, vi hälsar på kängurun! Vad kan hon drömma om?

The kangaroo jumps around the candy factory and fills her pouch. Even more of the blue sweets! And more lollipops! And chocolate!

When the dream is over, Lulu wants to go on another adventure. Come along, let's visit the knight! What could he be dreaming?

Kängurun hoppar genom godisfabriken och stoppar sin pung full. Ännu
fler av de blåa karamellerna! Och ännu fler klubbor! Och choklad!
När drömmen är slut vill Lulu uppleva ännu mer. Följ med, vi hälsar på
riddaren. Vad kan han drömma om?

The knight is having a cake fight with his dream princess. Oops! The whipped cream cake has gone the wrong way!

When the dream is over, Lulu wants to go on another adventure. Come along, let's visit the monkey! What could he be dreaming?

Riddaren har tårtkrig med sin drömprinsessa. Oj! Gräddtårtan missar!
När drömmen är slut vill Lulu uppleva ännu mer. Följ med, vi hälsar på
apan! Vad kan han drömma om?

Snow has finally fallen in Monkeyland. The whole barrel of monkeys is beside itself and getting up to monkey business.

When the dream is over, Lulu wants to go on another adventure. Come along, let's visit the pilot! In which dream could he have landed?

Äntligen har det snöat i aplandet! Hela apgänget är helt uppspelta och gör rackartyg.

När drömmen är slut vill Lulu uppleva ännu mer. Följ med, vi hälsar på piloten! I vilken dröm kan han ha landat i?

The pilot flies on and on. To the ends of the earth, and even farther, right on up to the stars. No other pilot has ever managed that.

When the dream is over, everybody is very tired and doesn't feel like going on many adventures anymore. But they'd still like to visit the lion cub.

What could she be dreaming?

Piloten flyger och flyger. Ända till världens ände och ännu längre, ända till stjärnorna. Ingen pilot har någonsin klarat av detta tidigare.
När drömmen är slut så är alla väldigt trötta och känner inte för att uppleva mycket mer. Men lejonungen vill de fortfarande hälsa på. Vad kan hon drömma om?

The lion cub is homesick and wants to go back to the warm, cozy bed.
And so do the others.

And thus begins ...

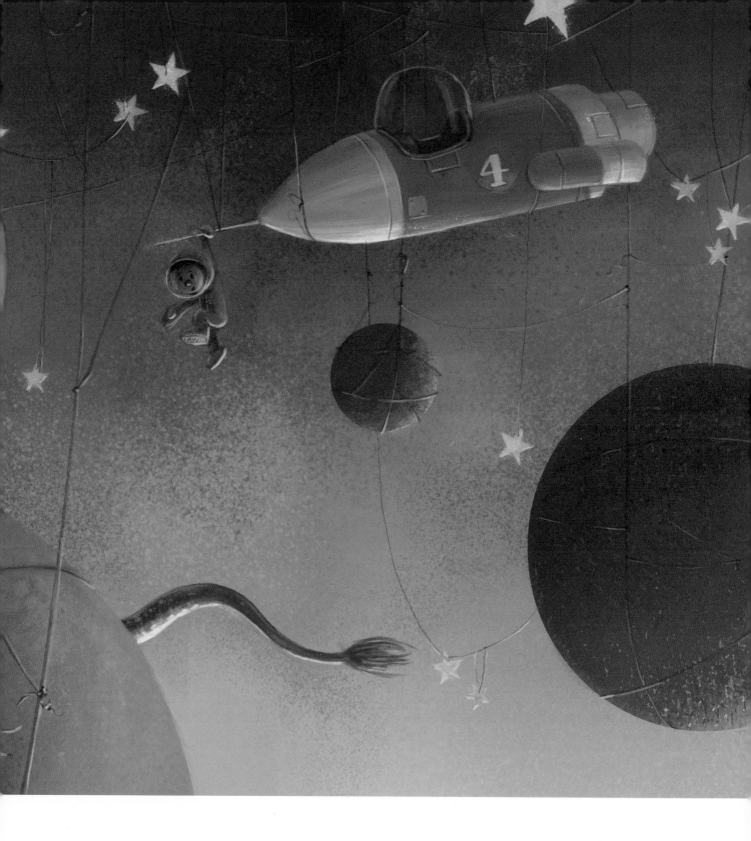

Lejonungen har hemlängtan och vill tillbaka till sin varma mysiga säng.
Och de andra med.

Och där börjar ...

... Lulu's
most beautiful dream.

... Lulus
allra vackraste dröm.

Foto: Ingrid Hagenreich

Cornelia Haas was born near Augsburg, Germany, in 1972. After completing her apprenticeship as a sign and light advertising manufacturer, she studied design at the Münster University of Applied Sciences and graduated with a degree in design. Since 2001 she has been illustrating childrens' and adolescents' books, since 2013 she has been teaching acrylic and digital painting at the Münster University of Applied Sciences.

Cornelia Haas föddes 1972 nära Augsburg (Tyskland). Efter utbildningen som skylt- och ljusreklamtillverkare studerade hon design vid Münster yrkeshögskola och utexaminerades som diplom designer. Sedan 2001 illusterar hon barn- och ungdomsböcker, sedan 2013 undervisar hon i akryl- och digitalmålning vid Münster yrkeshögskola.

www.cornelia-haas.de

Do you like drawing?

Here are the pictures from the story to color in:

www.sefa-bilingual.com/coloring

Enjoy!

Dear Reader,

Thanks for choosing my book! If you (and most of all, your child) liked it, please spread the word via a Facebook-Like or an email to your friends:

www.sefa-bilingual.com/like

I would also be happy to get a comment or a review. Likes and comments are great TLC for authors, thanks so much!

If there is no audiobook version in your language yet, please be patient! We are working on making all the languages available as audiobooks. You can check the „Language Wizard" for the latest updates:

www.sefa-bilingual.com/languages

Now let me briefly introduce myself: I was born in Stuttgart in 1960, together with my twin brother Herbert (who also became a writer). I studied French literature and a couple of languages in Paris, then medicine in Lübeck. However, my career as a doctor was brief because I soon discovered books: medical books at first, for which I was an editor and a publisher, and later non-fiction and children's books.

I live with my wife Kirsten in Lübeck in the very north of Germany; together we have three (now grown) children, a dog, two cats, and a little publishing house: Sefa Press.

If you want to know more about me, you are welcome to visit my website: **www.ulrichrenz.de**

Best regards,

Ulrich Renz

Lulu also recommends:

Sleep Tight, Little Wolf

For ages 2 and up

with audiobook for download

ISBN: 9783739906034

Tim can't fall asleep. His little wolf is missing! Perhaps he forgot him outside? Tim heads out all alone into the night – and unexpectedly encounters some friends...

Available in your languages?

▶ Check out with our „Language Wizard":

www.sefa-bilingual.com/language-wizard-wolf

Ulrich Renz · Marc Robitzky

The Wild Swans
De vilda svanarna

Based on a fairy tale by
Hans Christian Andersen

+ audio

English   bilingual   Swedish

ISBN: 9783739958989

The Wild Swans

Based on a fairy tale by Hans Christian Andersen

Recommended age: 4-5 and up

with audiobook for download

„The Wild Swans" by Hans Christian Andersen is, with good reason, one of the world's most popular fairy tales. In its timeless form it addresses the issues out of which human dramas are made: fear, bravery, love, betrayal, separation and reunion.

Available in your languages?

► Check out with our „Language Wizard":

www.sefa-bilingual.com/language-wizard-swans

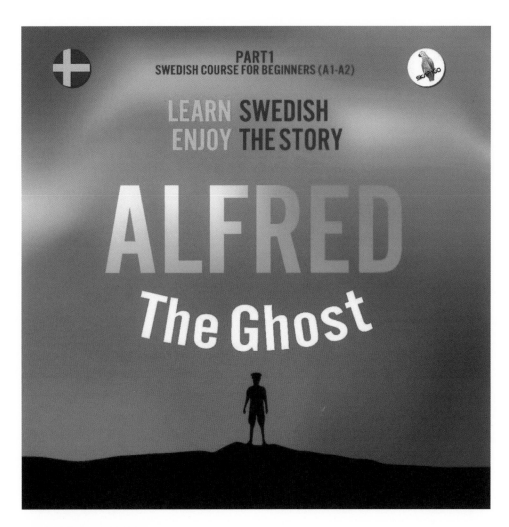

ISBN **9783945174104**

Learn Swedish with a fascinating story!

Would you like to read a fun story while getting serious instruction in grammar and vocabulary?

Then you should have a look at „Alfred the Ghost" by Skapago Publishing. You can learn Swedish with a coherent story that starts very simply, yet gets more and more advanced as the story progresses. Would you like to know how the story ends? If so.....you will just have to learn Swedish!

For more information and a free preview see

www.skapago.eu

More of me ...

Bo & Friends

- ▶ Children's detective series in three volumes. Reading age: 9+

- ▶ German Edition: „Motte & Co" ▶ www.motte-und-co.de

- ▶ Download the series' first volume, „Bo and the Blackmailers" for free!

www.bo-and-friends.com/free